beauty care
for
the tongue

beauty care
for
the tongue

Leroy Koopman

ZONDERVAN
PUBLISHING HOUSE
OF THE ZONDERVAN CORPORATION | GRAND RAPIDS. MICHIGAN 49506

Unless otherwise indicated, all Scripture is from the *Revised Standard Version* and is used by permission of the Division of Christian Education of the National Council of the Churches of Christ in the United States of America.

BEAUTY CARE FOR THE TONGUE

Tenth printing   March 1979
ISBN 0-310-26842-7

Printed in the United States of America

Contents

beauty care
for
the tongue

The Importance of a
Beautiful Tongue

How beautiful is your tongue?

Or haven't you ever really considered your tongue in terms of its attractiveness?

You don't look at it very often in the mirror.

You don't go on shopping trips for it.

You don't have a weekly appointment at the tongue beautician.

Avon and Revlon don't sell cosmetics for it.

You don't have to diet to get it back in shape.

Men don't ogle it or whistle at it or write poems about it.

It doesn't appear on the centerfold of *Playboy*.

Yet it is your tongue, more than the form of your face, or the dimensions of your figure, or the lavishness of your wardrobe, or the size of your income, which determines whether or not you are a beautiful person.

King Solomon was by no means a Puritan in his judgments on beauty, yet in his marvelous poem, Song of Solomon, he pays tribute to the beauty of the tongue: "Your lips are like a scarlet thread, and your words are delightful" (Song of Solomon 4:3 NEB).

The tongue can give new delights, year after year.

The tongue can make a plain person into a beautiful person.

The tongue can heal bruises and scrapes.

7

The tongue can soothe the agitated temper.

The tongue can give hope to the despondent soul.

The tongue can point the way to God.

The Bible compares it to the rudder of a ship — which, although it is relatively small, controls the direction of the entire vessel: "Look at the ships also; though they are so great and are driven by strong winds, they are guided by a very small rudder wherever the will of the pilot directs" (James 3:4). The Bible also compares it to a fire — of which a small spark can create a great holocaust: "So the tongue is a little member and boasts of great things. How great a forest is set ablaze by a small fire!" (James 3:5).

The tongue can make or break your marriage.

It can make your home a paradise or a desert.

It can draw your children to you in affection or send them away from you in disgust.

It can make and keep friends or lose them.

It can defend a good cause or allow an evil cause to go unchecked.

It can make the difference between hiring and firing.

It can heal a church or kill it.

It can attract people to Christ or send them away from Him.

It can honor God or curse Him.

It can save potential suicides, and it can drive people to self-destruction. As Proverbs 18:21 says, "Death and life are in the power of the tongue."

Your reputation will, in large part, be established by the use you make of your tongue. It will leave a lasting impression on people. It will label your character. The bystanders at the trial of Jesus said more than they realized when they said to Peter, "Your accent betrays you" (Matthew 26:73).

It's not an easy matter to cultivate an attractive tongue. "For every kind of beast and bird, of reptile and sea creature, can be tamed and has been tamed by humankind, but no human being can tame the tongue — a restless evil, full of deadly poison" (James 3:7, 8). The tongue is an ornery critter, wild as a bucking bronco. Just when we think we have it under control — its mighty energy harnessed, its wild nature tamed — the wild mustang spirit breaks out again, sending the snorting creature into a bucking spree, hooves flying, boards splintering, harness dangling, and dust choking.

How, then, can the tongue be brought under control? How can it be tamed and trained to become a thing of beauty and useful power?

This powerful organ can be made beautifully powerful only by bringing it under the control of an even greater power — the power of God's Holy Spirit.

Jesus promised, "You shall receive power when the Holy Spirit has come upon you" (Acts 1:8). When the Spirit came at Pentecost, the first object on earth that it used was the tongue! The disciples began to speak in languages that could be understood by the foreign Jews who were visiting in Jerusalem for the feast. Simon Peter — the same Peter who earlier had cursed and sworn before a servant girl while denying Christ — got up to give a sermon, and the Holy Spirit used his tongue so marvelously that three thousand people responded and were saved.

In 1 Corinthians 12:3 we read, "Therefore I

9

want you to understand that no one speaking by the Spirit of God ever says 'Jesus be cursed!' and no one can say 'Jesus is Lord' except by the Holy Spirit." It is the Spirit which transforms the cursing tongue into a confessing tongue.

The conclusion of the matter is this: your tongue cannot become a thing of beauty by your own efforts alone. It takes the superhuman work of the Holy Spirit.

This is not to say that your own effort is not needed. God has given you a mind and a will, and He expects you to use them. He requires that you assume responsibility over the marvelous instrument He has given you. He has revealed a wealth of information and advice on how to use the tongue, and He expects you to put it into practice.

BEAUTY EXERCISES

1. In addition to reading this lesson material and any other items your leader may assign, we are suggesting that you commit to memory just one scripture verse each week, for a total of four each month. Yes, we know that scripture memorization isn't the "in" thing right now; but we also remember what the psalmist said, "I have laid up thy word in my heart, that I might not sin against thee" (Psalm 119:11).

The verses will be printed under the section BREATH FRESHENERS. Just as you take mints along in your purse to sweeten your breath, take these verses along in your mind to sweeten your words. Your leader may ask that you repeat these verses together in unison at the monthly meeting.

2. Carefully study chapters 3 and 4 of the Book of James. This is the most sustained passage in

10

the Bible that deals specifically with the tongue. On a sheet of paper jot down all the items to which the tongue is compared (a horse's bit, a rudder, etc.). What is the significance of each of these analogies?

3. Reexamine your concept of beauty. What are you striving for most, inward beauty or outward beauty? What kind of beauty is most important in the eyes of the people you know and respect?

4. Include in your prayers a few sincere petitions for that important piece of flesh which lies between your teeth. Recognize that it is the Holy Spirit who can give it both discipline and power. Begin to yield your tongue to that Spirit.

BREATH FRESHENERS
Choice Tidbits to Chew On and Digest

First Week:
"So the tongue is a little member and boasts of great things. How great a forest is set ablaze by a small fire!" (James 3:5).

Second Week:
"For we all make many mistakes, and if any one makes no mistakes in what he says she is a perfect woman, able to bridle the whole body also" * (James 3:2).

Third Week:
"Death and life are in the power of the tongue" (Proverbs 18:21).

Fourth Week:
"Your lips are like a scarlet thread, and your words are delightful" (Song of Solomon 4:3, NEB).

---

* The original uses the masculine gender.

11

BEAUTY HINT #2

A Beautiful Tongue
Is a Silent Tongue

It was once said of a great linguist, "He could remain silent in seven different languages."

The Bible certainly isn't silent about the art of keeping silent.

Proverbs 10:19 says that "When words are many, transgression is not lacking, but he who restrains his lips is prudent."

Ecclesiastes says, in the well-known "a time to" passage, that there is a time to keep silent and a time to speak (Ecclesiastes 3:7). All too often we get our times mixed up; we speak when we ought to keep silent, and we keep silent when we ought to speak.

Psalm 4:4 teaches us to "commune with your own hearts on your beds, and be silent."

And it says in the letter of James: "Know this, my beloved brethren. Let every man be quick to hear, slow to speak, slow to anger" (James 1:19). Most of us do just the opposite — we are slow to hear and quick to speak.

It's true, isn't it, that so often when we are conversing with another person, we don't really listen to what she is saying. In fact, while the other person is speaking, we are thinking about what we are going to say in return. If both individuals are going through the same little ritual, we have the ludicrous situation of two people talking to themselves together. There is a sobering proverb: "A fool takes no pleasure in understanding, but only in expressing his opinion" (Proverbs 18:2).

How does one develop a beautiful tongue? The first exercise we suggest is this: initiate a program of *constructive silence*. It won't be easy, because it takes more muscle power to keep the tongue silent than to activate it.

Constructive Silence Eliminates Gossip

We ought to be "slow to speak" said James (1: 19). Why? Because much of what we are tempted to say has no constructive purpose. Much of it is just gossip — a mixture of truth, half-truth, and outright untruth — which hurts everyone and helps no one. Even if it is the truth, are you under an obligation to broadcast it to the world?

If you say nothing, no one can repeat it. When it comes to gossip, a beautiful tongue is a silent tongue.

Constructive Silence Promotes Harmony With Others

We could stay out of a lot of trouble with other people if we would relax our tongues a bit more. You may have noticed that James 1:19 places speech and anger close together: "Be . . . slow to speak, slow to anger."

We speak most impulsively when we are angry. We speak most rapidly when we are angry. We speak most unthinkingly when we are angry. Tempers and voices rise together. It's not the disagreement itself that leaves the scars after an argument; it's the words that were said in haste.

Another thing to consider: it's a well-known fact that we irritate people when we talk too much. Compulsive talkers find it difficult to keep friends. The good listener is more popular than the poor listener. It's simply common sense and good manners to refrain from monopolizing the conversation.

Constructive Silence Can Give You a Ministry to Others

Did you know that often you can be of great help to others simply by being a "sounding board" for them? People are troubled, or aged, or lonely, or making a decision, or simply need someone to care. You don't have to produce sage advice or magnificent words of wisdom; you just provide an open ear.

Occasionally a psychiatrist will admit that a major part of his therapy is simply listening while his patients speak their minds. And these folks are willing to pay $25 to $100 per hour just to have somebody listen without interrupting or arguing. The implication is that there is often no one at home who is willing to silence his tongue long enough to open his ears.

Church members often go to their pastors for precisely the same reason. They need someone who will listen. There have been times when I as a pastor have been thanked over and over again for "how much I have helped," when actually I had said hardly anything during the entire call.

Often extramarital affairs originate not because of unfulfilled passion or premeditated unfaithfulness, but because one person needed to talk and a friend happened to be willing to listen. Wives — listen!

Many of our personal problems could be solved so easily if we would just learn to listen! We could save hundreds of dollars on medical bills; we could enjoy happier marriages; we could contribute to the well-being of others, if we would just close our mouths and open our ears.

Constructive Silence Is Important in Our Relationship With God

Elijah expected God to reveal Himself in the great windstorm and in the earthquake and in the fire. Instead, He revealed Himself with a still, small voice (1 Kings 19:9-18). If Elijah hadn't kept quiet and listened intently, he wouldn't have heard God's message for himself and for Israel.

"Be still," says the Lord, "and know that I am God" (Psalm 46:10). "Be silent, all flesh, before the Lord," said the prophet Zechariah (Zechariah 2:13).

Prayer is to be a two-way conversation with God. Prayer is with the ears as well as with the mouth. Listen for the still, small voice. Give God a chance to get a word in — and give Him enough room so He doesn't have to get it in edgewise.

BEAUTY EXERCISES
To Help Relax Your Tongue

1. Make a call on an elderly person and give her an entire hour to talk about anything she wants to talk about.

2. After conversing with a friend, jot down as accurately as possible everything she said. In other words, check on how good you were as a listener.

3. Refrain from passing on a tempting tidbit of gossip, even though you think it won't hurt anyone. It's good discipline for the tongue (and it probably *would* hurt someone).

4. Listen carefully at the next discussion group you sit in on — whether it be a Sunday school class or a meeting of the Garden Club. Try to answer these questions: What percentage of the group members did 80 percent of the talking? Was it the ones who knew the most who did the most talking?

5. Next time you pray, give God equal time. If you pray for five minutes, remain silent for five minutes. If you pray ten minutes, remain silent ten minutes. After you have spoken to Him, let Him speak to you.

6. Resist the temptation to argue an unimportant point, even though you know you are right. Just be quiet about it and talk about something constructive instead. Or better yet, let somebody else talk about something constructive.

BREATH FRESHENERS

Caution: These may have a paralyzing effect on the tongue.

First Week:

"Know this, my beloved sisters. Let every woman be quick to hear, slow to speak, slow to anger" * (James 1:19).

Second Week:

"A fool takes no pleasure in understanding, but only in expressing her opinion" * (Proverbs 18:2).

Third Week:

"Be silent, all flesh, before the Lord" (Zechariah 2:13).

Fourth Week:

"(There is) a time to keep silence, and a time to speak" (Ecclesiastes 3:7).

---

* The original uses the masculine gender.

A Beautiful Tongue
Is an Appreciative Tongue

You all know how wonderful it is to be appreciated — to know that your sweat, worry, time, and tears had a happy effect on some life, and then to have that life respond with a gesture of thanks.

If it is important to you to *be appreciated*, then it is logical to assume that it is important to *appreciate*. It is, in fact, appreciative people who are most appreciated by others!

An appreciative tongue is so important that in America we set aside a special day in November to exercise it! Our Pilgrim fathers knew the value of an appreciative tongue. May we never abandon that part of our rich heritage.

An Appreciative Tongue
Exemplifies True Godliness

One of the surest signs of genuine godliness is a sincere sense of appreciation before the Almighty.

What, according to Romans 1, is the tragic fault of those who have drifted away from God? The answer is in verse 21: "For although they knew God they did not honor him as God or give thanks to him." Having refused to humbly acknowledge the Creator, they then proceeded to further insult Him by creating animalistic images of Him (vv. 22 and 23) and then degraded themselves further by giving their own bodies to the practice of immorality (vv. 24-27). But the root of it all was thanklessness.

God's greatest people have been appreciative people. King David devoted scores of his psalms to the theme of thankfulness (see Psalms 35:18; 65:1; 92:1; 108:1; 116:17). Paul began most of his letters with a statement of thanks (Romans 1:8; 1 Corinthians 1:4; Ephesians 1:15, 16). In his letters he also singled out certain people, such as Prisca and Aquila (Romans 16:3, 4) and Onesiphorus (2 Timothy 1:16-18) for special words of appreciation.

You no doubt recall the story in Luke 17:11-19 about the ten lepers healed by Jesus, only one of whom returned to give thanks. The nine who went on their way without so much as a backward glance received a blessing, that of physical healing. But the one with the appreciative tongue received an additional blessing: not only was he healed, but he got to know the Healer. Not only did he feel the power, but he became personally acquainted with the source. He found out that the Provider is also the Savior.

In this same story of the ten lepers we see the difference between genuine gratitude and just "feeling lucky." We can be sure that the nine who hurried off felt lucky. One can "feel lucky" all by one's self, without communication and without love for anyone. Appreciation always implies communication and a person-to-person relationship. Appreciation implies a bond of friendship. It indicates that a relationship is highly valued. This is why gratitude is so important in respect to

God; it indicates that there is a personal relationship between the individual and his God.

An Appreciative Tongue Will Put
Our Requests Into Perspective

"Have no anxiety about anything," says the letter, "but in everything by prayer and supplication *with thanksgiving* let your requests be made known to God" (Philippians 4:6).

A beautiful prayer will not only ask God for something new; it will thank Him for something old. A prayer *of* blessing will accompany a prayer *for* blessing.

Ask God for cake, if you will, but first thank Him for bread. Ask Him for victory over the power of sin, but also thank Him for deliverance from the guilt of sin. Ask Him for a happier home life, but thank Him first for a home. Ask Him for shoes, but also thank Him for feet.

An Appreciative Tongue Will Give
You a Better Home Life

It was the happy experience of the woman described in Proverbs 31 to be appreciated: "Her children rise up and call her blessed; her husband also, and he praises her" (vs. 28). No wonder she was such a remarkable person! She had a cheering section! In her home, the practice of personal appreciation was the accepted life-style.

An appreciative tongue acts as a love-bond for all relationships, and this is especially true in our homes.

Do you really want to make your husband feel that his life is worth living? Then appreciate him! And let him know about it!

Perhaps he has provided you with a comfortable

living. Perhaps he can afford only the modest things in life. No matter; *he provides*, and he works hard to earn his paycheck. Appreciate it.

Accentuate the positive. Instead of complaining about what you don't have, tell him you appreciate what you do have. Instead of harping about the old washing machine, emphasize how beautifully the new vacuum cleaner works. Even your "innocent" remarks about Mrs. Snelling's beautiful new clothes will probably be interpreted by him as a back-handed insult to his earning power (and it is, isn't it?). He'll become a better handler of the family finances if you compliment him on his successes. He'll become a better lover if you tell him how much you enjoy him. He'll become a better father if you verbally approve of the way he handled a particular discipline situation.

Loved ones tend to become what you say they are!

An Appreciative Tongue Will Change Your Perspective on Things

She who has learned to appreciate has learned to see the beautiful.

A vulture and a hummingbird are flying over the same desert. The vulture will find a decaying dead body, because that's what he is looking for. The hummingbird will find a beautiful flower, because that's what he is looking for. You will find what you want to find.

The appreciative customer at the check-out counter will be more inclined to notice the friendliness of the bag-packer than the grumpiness of the check-out girl. When working in the garden, the appreciative person will be happier over the strawberries than she will be disgusted with the weeds. When caring for the baby, she will talk more about the joy of seeing the child grow than she will complain about dirty diapers. When evaluating the neighbors, she will treasure more highly their friendliness than she will curse their noisy dog. In going to church, the appreciative woman will treasure more highly the truth of a sermon than she will deplore the preacher's nasal voice.

Appreciation will not eliminate all the ugliness, unrest, and uncertainty of life, but it will help you to cope with it and to enjoy it a great deal more.

BEAUTY EXERCISES

1. This month, compliment five or more of the following people, taking special note of their response to your appreciation. (Your group leader may ask you to report on this at the meeting.)

    a. The check-out girl at the supermarket, for her pleasant smile.

    b. The station attendant, for the extra-clean windshield.

    c. The waitress at the restaurant, for her efficiency.

    d. A Sunday school teacher, for her faithfulness.

    e. The organist, for an excellent prelude. (If you really want to shock her, compliment the postlude; no one ever seems to listen to that.)

    f. A neighbor, for not waking you up at 6:30 A.M. with his power mower.

    g. Your husband, for his uncanny ability to fix the toaster.

    h. Your mother, for her excellent gravy.

    i. _____ etc., etc.

2. When you pray, accompany each request with a related word of thanks. Discipline yourself not to ask for anything until you have first thanked Him for something.

3. Look for things to be thankful for, rather than for things to gripe about. Be like the hummingbird, not like the vulture. You'll be surprised to see a vast treasury of beauty, love, and strength that you never knew was there.

4. Begin each day this month by reciting one of this month's "Breath Fresheners." Make it more important than your first cup of coffee.

5. Read Psalms 90 to 106.

6. Pick out a person who seems to dislike you. Smother him (or her) with appreciation.

BREATH FRESHENERS
Don't You Wish Everybody Did?

First Week:

"O give thanks to the Lord, for he is good; for his steadfast love endures for ever!" (Psalm 107:1).

Second Week:

"Have no anxiety about anything, but in everything by prayer and supplication with thanksgiving let your requests be made known to God" (Philippians 4:6).

Third Week:

"For everything created by God is good, and nothing is to be rejected if it is received with thanksgiving; for then it is consecrated by the word of God and prayer" (1 Timothy 4:4, 5).

Fourth Week:

"Give thanks in all circumstances; for this is the will of God in Christ Jesus for you" (1 Thessalonians 5:18).

BEAUTY HINT #4

A Beautiful Tongue
Is a Witnessing Tongue

There are two extremes when it comes to witnessing for Christ. There are those who cannot enter into any kind of normal conversation without making a hard-sell pitch for the listener to be saved. Eventually they find that people begin avoiding them as if they had leprosy. On the other hand, there are those who never, never, never give the slightest indication that they are Christian believers and wouldn't have the foggiest idea what to say if someone asked them how to become one.

Most of us are somewhere in between these two extremes. There may be a few who ought to tone down a bit, but chances are that most of us are nearer to the second extreme than we are to the first. We may talk about our church, but we don't talk about our faith. We may talk about our minister, but we don't say much about our Savior. We pass up glorious opportunities to witness because we are afraid of what people will say — and because we haven't been taught what to say.

A Private Faith Must Also Be a Public Faith

Believing and confessing are Siamese twins. What the heart knows the tongue must say. "If you confess with your lips that Jesus is Lord," says the Bible, "and believe in your heart that God raised him from the dead, you will be saved"

23

(Romans 10:9). God needs public defenders far more than He needs secret disciples.

The phrase "Jesus is Lord" is apparently the earliest Christian creed, used by believers even before the so-called "Apostles' Creed." It doesn't contain a lot of systematic theology, but it contains a personal statement of what Jesus means to me: He is the Lord of my life, and He is my Lord because He is first of all my Savior.

A Witnessing Tongue Is Always Ready to Speak for Christ

"Always be prepared," says Peter, "to make a defense to any one who calls you to account for the hope that is in you" (1 Peter 3:15).

This presupposes a life that is literally beaming with hope; a life so unique that it causes people to ask, "I wonder what makes her so happy?" If your life is grumpy and morose, if your tongue is critical and nasty, no one is going to call on you to "account for the hope that is in you." A beautiful life and a beautiful tongue must go together in order to make a beautiful witness.

This verse, 1 Peter 3:15, gives us three important characteristics of a beautiful witnessing tongue.

First of all, it must be a *willing* tongue. Your tongue, says Peter, must "always be prepared" to make a defense of your hope.

A "defense" is simply the statement of a case.

You are, in a sense, a witness for the defense of Christ in the courtroom of the world. Everyone in the world is a jury member and must give a verdict; either he will find Jesus to be Savior, as claimed, or he will reject Him as a cheat and a fraud. In this courtroom you can give a personal testimony as to what kind of person you have found Him to be. You can tell about what He has done for you. You can tell of how you hope to share an eternity with Him. You can be, as it were, a "character witness."

Let us say, by way of illustration, that you are unjustly charged with a crime such as disorderly conduct. Your lawyer might be inclined to call to the witness stand various friends of yours who would be willing to vouch for your gentle and non-violent character. How would you feel if one by one your "friends" refused to take the witness stand, stating that they were "too busy" or "embarrassed by the publicity," or "afraid of the questions that might be asked"? How do you suppose Christ would feel if you, who profess to be His friend, back down with all kinds of excuses when called upon by the court of the world to "give an account for the hope that is in you"?

Secondly, the witnessing tongue must be a *gentle* tongue. No one can be an effective witness with a chip on her shoulder. The witnessing tongue must reflect the compassionate spirit of Christ as He dealt with the various kinds of sinners of His day. It must attract rather than antagonize, invite rather than threaten, and console rather than condemn. If the bridge of human friendship is blocked, the Gospel will not get across.

Thirdly, the witnessing tongue must be a *reverent* tongue. We understand this to mean reverence for God, reverance for the great truths which are being shared, and reverence for the personality of the other person. If there must be a debate, let it be in the spirit of promoting God's truth rather than gaining a victory. If you use scripture texts, use them accurately. Let the tone and spirit of what you say be found acceptable to Christ Himself.

A Witnessing Tongue Can Be Trained

There is a tremendous need for training in evangelism. Many people are not "prepared" in the sense of being willing, because they are not "prepared" in the sense of being trained. Every church ought to have an active program in which members are taught how to witness for Christ and then are given the opportunity to do so. Step-by-step procedures can be used. Scripture can be memorized. Christians should know how to "pull in the net" and call for a decision for Christ. There should be a definite schedule for calling on non-members. More experienced callers can train less-experienced callers.

If there is such a program in your church, join it. If there is not, see to it that there is.

A Witnessing Tongue Trusts in the Guidance of the Spirit

No one can really dispute the need for training in evangelism. Its necessity for self-confidence and for competence cannot be doubted. Yet, let us not think that it is all up to us. It is God's Holy Spirit who gives power to the witnessing tongue. Without the Spirit we are helpless. Our carefully executed procedures will fall lifeless to the ground unless we receive His help.

There are times when our best-learned techniques must be abandoned, when our careful plans must be thrown aside, and when we will hear ourselves speaking words that are completely spontaneous and unrehearsed. This is evidence of the power of the Holy Spirit. No one was more careful than Jesus in instructing His disciples. Yet He also pointed out that they couldn't possibly be prepared for every situation they would encounter. He told them they must not fear the unknown and the unplanned-for, for the Spirit would help them: "When they deliver you up, do not be anxious how you are to speak or what you are to say; for what you are to say will be given to you in that hour" (Matthew 10:19).

Even in ugly situations a witnessing tongue is a beautiful tongue.

BEAUTY EXERCISES
For Christ's Public Defenders

1. Enroll in some good program for the training of lay witnesses. This may be offered by your local church, or by an interdenominational group, or by a neighboring church. The point is — *become trained.*

2. Become involved in some aspect of your congregational outreach. You may volunteer for "front line" service as an evangelistic caller or for the less rigorous duties of the "support troops" (mailing brochures, distributing tracts, etc.) — but *do something.*

3. Invite a new Christian into your home for coffee, for a social evening, or for dinner. Satan works hard on new believers, and your friendship and support are very important.

4. Talk to your pastor about the evangelistic thrust of your congregation. Commend him for what has been done. Help him to evaluate strengths and weaknesses. Point out needs. Encourage him to be bold in initiating new approaches. Offer your services.

5. Be a constant witness. This doesn't mean you should talk about nothing but Christ. It does mean your speech and conduct should display both the love and ethic of Christ. It does mean you can be aware of the openings others give you to talk about faith. It does mean you can create your own opportunities for witness.

6. Bring a new child to Sunday school every week this month.

BREATH FRESHENERS
To Add a Hint of More Than Mint

First Week:

"If you confess with your lips that Jesus is Lord and believe in your heart that God raised him from the dead, you will be saved" (Romans 10: 9).

Second Week:

"Always be prepared to make a defense to any one who calls you to account for the hope that is in you, yet do it with gentleness and reverence" (1 Peter 3:15).

Third Week:

"When they deliver you up, do not be anxious how you are to speak or what you are to say; for what you are to say will be given to you in that hour" (Matthew 10:19).

Fourth Week:

"Go therefore and make disciples of all nations, baptizing them in the name of the Father and of the Son and of the Holy Spirit, teaching them to observe all that I have commanded you; and lo, I am with you always, to the close of the age" (Matthew 28:19, 20).

A Beautiful Tongue
Is a Clean Tongue

A certain toothpaste container says that its product is valuable if used with a "conscientiously applied program of oral hygiene."

What America needs more than it realizes is a conscientiously applied program of oral hygiene. And it's not the kind that comes out of a toothpaste tube or that is assured if you see your dentist once every six months. It's the kind that only Christ can give when He applies His unique cleansing action to the entire oral cavity.

America has an X-rated mouth.

Profanity is everywhere —

— From the ghetto to the vice-president's office.
— From the PTA to the Senate.
— From the schoolyard to the Convention of Vacuum Cleaner Salesmen.
— From the kitchen to the beauty shop.
— From the drive-in movie to the Broadway stage.

Yes, and even from the Ministerial Association to the pulpit; for the use of profanity supposedly labels the radical chic clergyman as "one of the boys" and expresses his new "liberation."

And speaking of liberation — some women believe that women's lib has set them free to use the same swear words their husbands use. That's liberation?

A study of profanity at Wayne State University revealed that college students use one off-color word for every fourteen. That's better than adults, who use one bad word in every ten.

Few people seem to be concerned about dirty tongues. They're concerned about air pollution and water pollution and earth pollution — but the aren't concerned about pollution of the sound waves.

The words of Jesus are appropriate in this age in which we are so concerned about the purity of what we eat, breathe, and drink: "Not what goes into the mouth defiles (pollutes) a man, but what comes out of the mouth, this defiles (pollutes) a man" (Matthew 15:11).

We'd like to share a few more things that the Bible says about a clean tongue.

A Clean Tongue Shows Reverence for God

"You shall not take the name of the Lord your God in vain; for the Lord will not hold him guiltless who takes his name in vain" (Exodus 20:7).

Society may think he's cute. But the Bible says that God will not hold him guiltless. Why?

Because a name is more than a name. It represents a person. When Sally Smith bitterly complains that because of gossip she has "lost her good name," she is not saying that someone has harmed the letters S A L L Y S M I T H. She is saying that someone has harmed her reputation, besmirched her character before others, and has hurt her to the core of her personality.

Similarly, to abuse the name of God is to abuse more than a few letters of the alphabet. It is to abuse a Person. It is to show extreme disrespect for the Holy One. It is to harm God's reputation.

It is to attack His very Being. It is to play lightly with His character.

A *Clean Tongue Displays Reverence*
for All Things Holy, Personal,
Private, and Important

A clean tongue is a beautiful tongue because it breathes reverence — reverence for all things good and beautiful; reverence for life itself; reverence for the way God has made us.

She who speaks with a clean tongue expresses a sensitivity to the spiritual.

She who refuses to use the common four-letter words for sexual realities implies a high esteem for that relationship. The profane tongue implies animalism and contempt.

She who speaks carefully of words like "heaven," "hell," and "damn," expresses reverence for the respective realities of those words, whether happy or dreadful. She who uses them indiscriminately is saying that she either denies or ignores their existence.

A *Clean Tongue Displays a Good Stewardship*
of the God-Given Talent of Clear
Concise, and Colorful Speech

The ability to communicate with the tongue is one of God's greatest gifts to the human race. The Christian believer realizes that speech, like her other talents and abilities, is to be used and educated and perfected as a part of her stewardship on earth.

Any ignoramus can swear. It takes no special talent to use cuss words. A parrot or myna bird can learn to swear quite proficiently. Limited word power often reflects limited brain power.

The clean-tongued person, on the other hand, is more than likely one who has consciously sought for original, colorful, and clear ways of expressing herself. She will avoid clichés in speech, seeking to get out of the habit of using "flat" and overused words (and there is no cliché quite as trite as a swear word). When she speaks, she really tries to *communicate;* she is not content to use the same invectives that she might, in a fit of rage, say to herself in an empty room.

A Clean Tongue Is, by Its Very Rarity, a Witnessing Tongue

Profanity is so common today that its very absence is distinctive. The person who has a clean tongue stands out in a group simply because she is a rarity.

Hopefully, your Christian witness will be far more explicit than that, but the mere absence of gutter words in your speech will label you as a person with certain convictions. Others will be strongly suspicious that you are a Christian believer and may even begin to excuse or curtail their own foul speech in your presence.

BEAUTY EXERCISES

To Include in Your Conscientiously Applied Program of Oral Hygiene

1. Are you continuing to memorize your "Breath Fresheners"? Really, now — they're not that difficult. Remember also to review all the verses you have learned earlier.

2. If your children use vulgar or profane language, don't allow it to go undisciplined and unchecked. The old "soap treatment" may sound silly, but it works!

3. Incidentally, check to see where your children are learning those words. Could it be in your own home?

4. To someone who is profuse in misusing the name of Jesus, say, "That's a good friend of mine you're talking about. Would you like to know more about Him?"

5. Remember to forget the smutty story you heard yesterday.

6. Even if you don't swear blatantly, check on the slang words you use — like "heavens," "darn," and "gosh."

BREATH FRESHENERS
To Keep Your Breath Clean

First Week:

"You shall not take the name of the Lord your God in vain; for the Lord will not hold him guiltless who takes his name in vain" (Exodus 20:7).

Second Week:

"I am the Lord, that is my name; my glory I give to no other" (Isaiah 42:8).

Third Week:

"Not what goes into the mouth defiles a woman, but what comes out of the mouth, this defiles a woman" * (Matthew 15:11).

Fourth Week:

"Let no evil talk come out of your mouths, but only such as is good for edifying, as fits the occasion, that it may impart grace to those who hear" (Ephesians 4:29).

---

* The original uses the masculine gender.

A Beautiful Tongue
Is a Kind Tongue

One of the most famous chapters of the entire Bible begins with these words: "If I speak in the tongues of men and of angels, but have not love, I am a noisy gong or a clanging cymbal" (1 Corinthians 13:1).

Cymbals have their place in an orchestra, but can you imagine the insanity they would cause if they were crashed constantly throughout an entire symphony?

Clanging gongs have their place in life — to wake us up, to warn us of fire, and to tell school classes that the period is over — but when they "stick," the sound becomes deafening and irritating.

Such is the sound of a voice without kindness. It may speak with beautiful eloquence, perfect diction, erudite intelligence, and syrupy sweetness. Yes, it may even speak in unknown tongues. But if it does not speak with genuine love, it emits but a garbled sound of irritating disharmony.

Jesus taught that there is one word that summarizes the entire Law: "You shall love the Lord your God . . . you shall love your neighbor" (Mark 12:30, 31). Love summarizes both the contents and the spirit of the Ten Commandments. The woman who speaks lovingly has made good progress in keeping God's holy Law.

A Kind Tongue Helps to Make a House a Home

We turn once again to Proverbs 31, that remarkable and still-timely vignette of a truly wonderful wife and mother. She is faithful, ambitious, intelligent, and generous. But she is more than that: she is kind. The beauty of her person is enhanced by the kindness of her words. "She opens her mouth with wisdom, and the teaching of kindness is on her tongue" (Proverbs 31:26). It is no wonder that a few verses later it says, "Her children rise up and call her blessed; her husband also, and he praises her" (vs. 28).

It is with kindness as it is with most good things: the place to begin is in the home.

Many, if not most, family problems could be solved or at least eased by a kind tongue. A little kindness goes a long way when your husband comes home from work — hot, tired, and irritable. A little kindness can solve a lot of math problems when Junior becomes disgusted with his homework. A little kindness saves many tears when Sally comes home crying because "I'm so ugly and nobody likes me and I'll never get a boyfriend."

A Kind Tongue Overcomes Speech Problems

Some people feel self-conscious when they speak. They think they say "dumb things," or have a peculiar accent, or have a voice that is pitched too high or too low, or have a small vocabulary, or say the wrong thing at the wrong time. If you feel this way, the gift of kindness may do more for you than a college course in public speaking. If you speak in love, all the alleged imperfections (supposed or real) simply become a harmony to the melody of kindness.

A Kind Tongue Supplements a Truthful Tongue

The Bible says in Ephesians that it's not enough just to speak the truth. We are to speak the truth "in love" (Ephesians 4:15).

Perhaps your husband acts boorish when he cracks his knuckles in public. Tell him the truth — but tell the truth in love.

Perhaps your friend is inviting tragedy by becoming too friendly with the plumber. Tell her the truth, and tell it to her soon (see James 5:19, 20), but tell it to her with kindness.

Perhaps the cultist who calls on your door is teaching a false doctrine. Show him the truth — but do it in love, without a slammed door and nasty remarks.

A Kind Tongue Promotes Peace

The Apostle Peter (who, by the way, had to struggle with a boistrous and unruly tongue) says, "Do not return evil for evil or reviling for reviling; but on the contrary bless, for to this you have been called, that you may obtain a blessing. For he that would love life and see good days, let him keep his tongue from evil and his lips from speaking guile" (1 Peter 3:9,10).

According to the letter of James, the tongue is like a wild horse, difficult to bridle and control. There is, however, one bit that will control the tongue. This is a bit of love.

We need a bit of love at all times, but we especially need it during times of personal antagonism. It's relatively easy to be kind to others when they are kind to us. The real test comes when we are provoked.

It's easy to be kind when hubby comes home

with flowers; it's not so easy when he comes home criticizing the tasteful way you have rearranged the furniture.

It's easy to smile at the customer who is satisfied; it's harder when she blames you for the high price tags.

It's easy to be kind when your neighbor is sweet and minds her own business; it's not so easy when she implies that you are raising a brood of undisciplined little delinquents.

The kind tongue is the kind of tongue that revealed Jesus as such an extraordinary person. "When he was reviled, he did not revile in return" (1 Peter 2:23). He loved the world He came to save to such an extent that He controlled the impulse to speak out in anger against the very people who were seeking to kill Him. Among His dying words were words of kindness: "Father, forgive them; for they know not what they do" (Luke 23: 34).

A Kind Tongue Is a Positive Witness for Christ

A woman of this author's acquaintance is well known in her church as an articulate leader at women's meetings and as an impressive leader in prayer. She is also known by the postmen, the deliverymen, the garbage men, the policemen, the service station men, and the paper boys of the neighborhood as "Mrs. Complainer" (they usually use a more descriptive word). For all her angelic utterances, she is a poor testimony to the transforming love of Jesus Christ. Her beautiful sounds are no more than clanging gongs and clashing cymbals.

The advice of Colossians 4:5, 6 is appropriate: "Conduct yourselves wisely toward outsiders, making the most of the time. Let your speech always be gracious, seasoned with salt."

BEAUTY EXERCISES
For the Development of a Kind Tongue

1. Choose a person you dislike. Then speak, call, or write to her (or him), doing your best to be genuinely kind. You don't have to overact, but do exhibit a gracious and positive attitude.

2. Next time you see your newspaper boy, speak kindly to him, no matter how many times he has thrown your paper under the bushes. (It might also improve his aim). Do likewise with the postman, garage man, check-out girl, delivery-man, etc.

3. Hold your tongue the next time you are provoked. Try to understand why the other person acts that way. Smother, don't fan, the potential quarrel.

4. Discuss with a few teenagers (preferably your own, if you have them) what impresses them most and what disillusions them most about adult Christians. How important to them are such items as kindness and love?

5. Be ready to share your friendship at a church meeting.

6. Write an original paraphrase of 1 Corinthians 13:1-3. Be creative and down-to-earth. You might try "A housewife's version of 1 Corinthians 13" or "A secretary's version . . ." or "A school-teacher's version . . ." or "A retiree's version. . . ."

BREATH FRESHENERS
For a Mouth That's Always Pleasant

First Week:

"If I speak in the tongues of men and of angels,

but have not love, I am a noisy gong or a clanging cymbal" (1 Corinthians 13:1).

Second Week:

"Be kind to one another, tenderhearted, forgiv-
ing one another, as God in Christ forgave you"
(Ephesians 4:32).

Third Week:

"She opens her mouth with wisdom, and the
teaching of kindness is on her tongue" (Proverbs
31:26).

Fourth Week:

"From the same mouth come blessing and cursing. My sisters, this ought not to be so" * (James
3:10).

---

* The original uses the masculine gender.

A Beautiful Tongue Is a Tongue That Does Not Gossip

This writer has heard people confess almost every sin there is, plus a few more. But he has never heard anyone admit to gossiping.

Perhaps it's because gossiping is so common that we don't realize we are doing it. Perhaps it's because we think we have excused ourselves by preceding gossip with such phrases as "I don't mean to talk about her, but . . ." and "Don't tell anyone else about this. . . ." Perhaps it's because if we would admit it, we might feel obligated to stop it.

The practice of gossip is one of the most subtle and common diseases of the tongue. It attacks both old and young, male and female, married and unmarried. It is a highly communicable disease (pardon the pun), and it is a sickness which leaves ugly scars.

Gossip Is Irretrievable

It has been said that letting the cat out of the bag is easy enough; the difficult part is trying to get it back in again.

Once a rumor is started, it is almost impossible to stop it. We may be sorry about it, and we may be forgiven by God for it, but we cannot undo the consequences.

Depend on this: the words you say about others will eventually get back to them. The Book of

Ecclesiastes has an interesting way of putting it: "Even in your thought, do not curse the king, nor in your bedchamber curse the rich; for a bird of the air will carry your voice, or some winged creature tell the matter" (10:20). What the writer is saying is that it's almost impossible to defame someone without that person somehow hearing about it. The means may be so mysterious that we accuse the very birds, but the message gets through.

"He who repeats a matter alienates a friend," says the Book of Proverbs (17:9). You may not think the friend will hear, but she always does.

A good rule to follow: If you wouldn't say it to her face, don't say it.

Gossip Is Unloving

No one can gossip about someone and truly love that person at the same time.

The second great commandment is to love our neighbor as ourselves. Even if the tales we tell succeed in passing the test of truthfulness, they still must pass the test of love. It is at this point that our conversation often "flunks out."

According to the great love chapter, 1 Corinthians 13, one of the characteristics of love is that it "does not rejoice at wrong, but rejoices in the right" (13:6). Phillips translates the phrase in this way: "It does not keep account of evil or gloat over the wickedness of other people. On the contrary, it is glad with all good men when truth prevails." The New English Bible lends still further light: "Love keeps no score of wrongs; does not gloat over other men's sins, but delights in the truth."

A substantial part of gossip is gloating over the

41

sins, faults, and idiosyncrasies of other people. Love, according to the Word of God, denies that luxury to our egos. Love will rejoice in telling good news and will refrain from wallowing in that which is bad.

What does the Bible say we are to do when a fellow believer falls into sin? Does it say we should spread the news all over town? Please refer to Galatians 6:1: "Brethren, if a man is overtaken in any trespass, you who are spiritual should restore him in a spirit of gentleness. Look to yourself, lest you too be tempted."

Four Reasons Why We Gossip

1. *We gossip because we lack healthy self-confidence and self-respect.*

It is when we feel insecure and threatened that we are most likely to spread ugly gossip about others. By rubbing some of the glitter from someone else's crown, we believe our own will shine more brightly. By cutting others down, we think we will feel taller.

The solution, then, is not merely to stop downgrading others; it is to begin upgrading yourself. Jesus said, "You shall love your neighbor as yourself" (Matthew 22:39). He didn't say *instead* of yourself; He said *as* yourself. He implied that you can't really accept your neighbor until you accept yourself. You must be a precious and valuable person, or God wouldn't have created you in His own image, sent His Son to die for you, promised the power of His Spirit in your life, and prepared a place for you to live with Him forever!

2. *We gossip because we haven't sufficiently*

stimulated our minds with more important things.

Says Charles Allen in *God's Psychiatry:* "Those of great minds discuss ideas, people of mediocre minds discuss events, and those of small minds discuss other people."[1]

One positive solution to gossip is to involve your mind with better and more important things. Be informed about world events and their significance. Read good books — nonfiction as well as fiction. Flip the TV dial from a situation comedy or soap opera to a talk show, a debate, or a documentary. Take an interest in the great social challenges of our time, such as race and poverty, and be able to discuss them intelligently.

3. *We gossip because we are idle.*

The housewife has made the beds and washed the dishes. It's not time to get lunch ready yet, and the soap operas don't come on until afternoon, so she spends an hour on the phone with a friend — talking about you know who.

The retiree has pulled all the weeds, and the mail won't be here for three hours, so she seeks out a neighbor for the latest news.

It's not a new story. Paul observed that widows in the church often did not have enough to do, so they learned to be "idlers, gadding about from house to house, and not only idlers but gossips and busybodies, saying what they should not" (1 Timothy 5:13).

There's nothing wrong with good fellowship. But all too often the ladies indulge in gossip-by-

---

[1] Charles L. Allen, *God's Psychiatry*, Fleming H. Revell Company, 1953, p. 75.

43

the-hour simply because they have nothing more valuable to do. One of the best cures for gossip is to get so busy doing something constructive that you just don't have time to worry about the private business of others.

4. *We gossip because we are in the habit of gossiping.*

Many a student who has been away at college for some time is shocked when he returns home — shocked at the intensity and volume of his parents' gossip. When living at home he had simply accepted it as "normal," but now that he has been away for awhile he sees it in a new perspective. Perhaps a tape recorder secretly placed in the kitchen or living room would shock us into realizing how gossip has become habitual with us.

BEAUTY EXERCISES
Designed to Eliminate Excess Flap

1. Before you pass along any story, check with the subject of the story to see if it is true. If, for instance, you hear that Pat Brown is stepping out on her husband, check with Pat Brown. This may accomplish one of two things: it may curtail your talk, and it may curtail Pat Brown's extracurricular activities.

2. Test the stories you hear by Philippians 4:8:
    Is it true?
    Is it honorable?
    Is it just?
    Is it pure?
    Is it lovely?
    Is it gracious?

If it passes all these tests, then by all means get on the telephone and pass it on!

3. Discuss some possible cures for gossiping. Talk it over with your husband and your children.

4. Next time you are with your friends at coffee, mutually agree to talk about anything at all *except* other people. Make a rule that the first offender has to pay some penalty, such as paying a quarter or providing the cookies at the next get-together. It may sound silly, but it will keep you aware.

BREATH FRESHENERS
For More Sparkling Conversations

First Week:
   "For lack of wood the fire goes out; and where there is no whisperer, quarreling ceases" (Proverbs 26:20).

Second Week:
   "He who repeats a matter alienates a friend" (Proverbs 17:9).

Third Week:
   "Finally, brethren, whatever is true, whatever is honorable, whatever is just, whatever is pure, whatever is lovely, whatever is gracious, if there is any excellence, if there is anything worthy of praise, think about these things" (Philippians 4:8).

Fourth Week:
   "(Love) . . . does not rejoice at wrong, but rejoices in the right" (1 Corinthians 13:6).

A Beautiful Tongue
Is a Truthful Tongue

A beautiful tongue is a truthful tongue because God, who invented the tongue, designed it to tell the truth. "Behold," says the psalmist, "thou desirest truth in the inward being" (Psalm 51:6). "Lying lips are an abomination to the Lord" (Proverbs 12:22). The ninth commandment calls for a truthful tongue: "You shall not bear false witness against your neighbor" (Exodus 20:16).

God is such a stickler for the truth because He is a God of truth. "God is not man, that he should lie, or a son of man, that he should repent. Has he said, and will he not do it? Or has he spoken, and will he not fulfill it?" (Numbers 23:19). Falsehood is the very antithesis of all that He is; therefore He hates it. His enemy, Satan, is called "the father of lies" (John 8:44). Murderers, idolaters, and others will join the liars in the "lake that burns with fire and sulphur, which is the second death" (Revelation 21:8). The lying tongue will come to a rather ugly end!

Lying is one of the worst forms of moral ugliness. It was a lie that caused our first parents to sin in the Garden of Eden. It was lies that brought about the sudden deaths of Ananias and Sapphira (Acts 5:1-11). It was lies that pinned Jesus to the cross.

More money is stolen by the tip of the tongue than by the point of a gun. Burglars may steal their thousands, but liars steal their tens of thousands — by padded expense accounts, misrepresented goods, altered records, false diagnosis of automobile and appliance troubles, and various confidence schemes.

There is little that breaks down the mutual confidence and respect of home life more quickly than the discovery of a lie. It says of the "ideal wife" in Proverbs 31 that "the heart of her husband trusts in her" (v. 11). Mutual trust is the silent and unseen oxygen that fuels the fires of love.

Probably most of us are careful to avoid outright and blatant lies. It is more likely to be the subtle untruths that keep our tongues from being as beautiful as they can be. It is these subtle untruths that will occupy us in this discussion.

A Truthful Tongue Avoids Half-truths

There are many ways of avoiding the truth. One of them is to tell only part of the truth. "Honey, a truck ran into my back fender at the intersection of 4th and Grove." That's true of course — but the other half of the truth is that the truck went through a green light and you went through a red one.

Another way to tell a half-truth is to combine truth and falsehood in one statement, thus making the falsehood more plausible: "She has been acting grumpy lately; she must be angry with me over something." The first part of the statement may be entirely true and the second part entirely false. Yet when they are placed side by side, the false is made to sound true.

A Truthful Tongue Speaks Up to Defend the Truth

A person can sometimes tell a lie merely by keeping silent. Jesus was condemned by lies; but He also was condemned because no one stood up before Pilate to tell the truth and set the record straight.

Over coffee after a women's meeting someone speculates that since Jean Simpson has missed two meetings in a row, "she's probably mad about something again." You don't really care for Jean Simpson, and you know that she often does get angry about little things. But you also know that she's visiting a sister in Chicago. If you say nothing, you are implying consent to the unkind judgment.

A Truthful Tongue Distinguishes Between Fact and Opinion

The story is being circulated in the community that John Meredith left college because he was caught smoking marijuana. The truth is that John quit college because he couldn't make the academic requirements. This talk about marijuana was somebody's educated guess. In the mysterious chemistry of gossip, opinion is a volatile substance which readily crystallizes into "fact" when mixed with a little saliva.

Every day we hear opinions stated as facts. "She certainly is unfriendly." "He is a poor minister." "You can't trust him." But these are personal viewpoints only; they are apt to be biased and one-sided. They would be more accurately stated, "I think that. . . ." The person with a beautiful tongue has trained herself to separate fact from implication, opinion, deduction, and innuendo.

A Truthful Tongue Is Careful
About Absolute Statements

"Henry," the wife cries, "you *never* talk to me any more." That's not quite the truth, is it? It's the kind of exaggerated statement that so often cuts to the heart.

"You are *always* so ungrateful."

"All you ever think about is sex."

"You're just like your mother."

"We never go out any more."

"Our marriage has been miserable for eleven years."

"I don't have anything to wear."

Not only will you be less untruthful if you cut out the absolute words such as "always" and "never," but you'll get along a lot better with your loved ones.

A Truthful Tongue Speaks
the Truth About Oneself

It's perhaps (notice I used the word *perhaps*) just as easy to be dishonest about yourself as to be untruthful about others.

How easily we justify our prejudices, excuse our mistakes, defend our bad judgments, and explain why we have failed! As the teenager said to his mother after she had finished giving him a lecture on some misdemeanor, "Mother, why do you suppose I do these things? Is it heredity or environment?"

On the other hand, it is also easy to do injustice to the truth by underrating ourselves. So often we fail unnecessarily, and we fail because we have told ourselves a lie. We say, "I can't do it," or "I'm just not smart enough," or "People will just laugh at me," or "I'll make a fool of myself."

God gave you talents, vitality, personality, and strength. Don't lie about what God gave you!

A Truthful Tongue Is Careful About "White Lies"

Most of us will agree that almost always it is best to tell the truth. But we also know there are borderline cases, the "white lies" which are meant for good.

What about the resident of Holland, for instance, who during World War II gave refuge to Jews? Was he obligated to tell the truth to the Gestapo? Most of us would agree that in this case the commandment to love takes precedence over the letter of the law.

What about some borderline cases?

The husband who tells his wife that her new dress is beautiful, even though he thinks it isn't?

The housewife who tells the mysterious stranger at the door that her husband will be home in ten minutes?

The medical doctor and the patient's family who do not tell the patient he has an inoperable cancer?

The parents who tell their children that Aunt Jenny went away on a long vacation, when in reality she ran off with the butcher?

No doubt you will wish to consider these questions at the meeting. On what basis do you decide the answer?

Remember, a beautiful tongue is a truthful tongue.

BEAUTY EXERCISES

1. Keep a notebook record of falsehoods, half-truths, and assorted opinions which are passed on to you as "truth" this month. Include such items as —

- the dogmatic statement that a radio preacher vowed was the only possible interpretation of some obscure passage in the prophecy of Ezekiel.
- what the garage man said was wrong with your car.
- the claims made by a television commercial.
- the excuses your children gave for not practicing the piano.
- the incorrect weight printed on the meat or fruit package at the supermarket.

2. Before quoting another person or repeating her opinion, check with her first, asking, "Did I understand you right?" or "Is this what you really meant?"

3. Be careful of your statements. Discipline yourself to tell the truth and only the truth. Don't exaggerate it, minimize it, twist it, or mix it with a pinch of anything else.

4. Be careful of your actions. Tell with your face what you are thinking in your mind and saying with your lips. If you disagree, don't nod your head. If you are concerned, don't try to act ho-hum. If you are unconcerned, don't make a pretense of being excited.

5. Don't do anything that you are ashamed to tell the truth about!

BREATH FRESHENERS
Containing a Drop of Truth Syrup

First Week:
"You shall not bear false witness against your neighbor" (Exodus 20:16).

Second Week:
"Lying lips are an abomination to the Lord, but

those who act faithfully are his delight" (Proverbs 12:22).

Third Week:

"Behold, thou desirest truth in the inward being; therefore teach me wisdom in my secret heart" (Psalm 51:6).

Fourth Week:

"Therefore, putting away falsehood, let every one speak the truth with her neighbor, for we are members one of another"* (Ephesians 4:25).

---

* The original uses the masculine gender.

BEAUTY HINT #9

A Beautiful Tongue Is
a Contented Tongue

Why were the Israelites who escaped from the
slave camps of Egypt not allowed to enter the
Promised Land? Why did their bones lie white
in the desert? Was it not because of their complaining tongues?

> And the Lord said to Moses and to Aaron,
> "How long shall this wicked congregation
> murmur against me? I have heard the mur-
> murings of the people of Israel, which they
> murmur against me. Say to them, 'As I live,'
> says the Lord, 'what you have said in my
> hearing I will do to you: your dead bodies
> shall fall in this wilderness; and all of your
> number, numbered from twenty years old and
> upward, who have murmured against me, not
> one shall come into the land where I swore
> that I would make you dwell, except Caleb
> the son of Jephunneh, and Joshua the son of
> Nun'" (Numbers 14:26-30).

"What causes wars, and what causes fightings
among you?" asked James. "Is it not your passions
that are at war in your members? You desire and
do not have; so you kill. And you covet and cannot obtain; so you fight and wage war" (James
4:1, 2).

Among those who will be dealt with most harshly at the last judgment, says Jude, are the "grumblers" and the "malcontents" (Jude 16).

The Apostle Paul had plenty to complain about. He had a "thorn in the flesh" that must have been painful and inconvenient. Time and time again he was beaten, shipwrecked, forcibly evicted, and persecuted. He spent two years languishing in a prison without any formal charges being lodged against him. Yet he was no complainer. "I have learned," he said, "in whatever state I am, to be content. I know how to be abased, and I know how to abound; in any and all circumstances I have learned the secret of facing plenty and hunger, abundance and want. I can do all things in him who strengthens me" (Philippians 4:11-13). In this same letter, written from a prison cell, the words "joy" and "rejoice" appear no less than thirteen times in five short chapters.

"There is great gain," Paul said to Timothy, "in godliness with contentment" (1 Timothy 6:6).

"Rob no one by violence or by false accusation," John the Baptist told the soldiers, "and be content with your wages" (Luke 3:14).

"Be content with what you have," said the writer of the letter to the Hebrews, "for he has said 'I will never fail you nor forsake you'" (Hebrews 13:5).

A grumbling and complaining tongue is an ugly tongue.

A contented tongue is a beautiful tongue.

A Contented Tongue Handles Illness With Courage and Quiet Strength

I am sure you have all met the kind of woman who never gets asked "How are you?" The uninitiated soul who unknowingly asks that fatal question is treated to a lengthy and gory discourse on the length of her recent operation, the amount of blood lost, and the precise medical terms for at least half of the organs in her body. To say nothing of last year's arthritis, this year's sinus trouble, and her sister's miscarriage.

You have also no doubt visited people whom you knew were in great pain, yet they maintained a spirit of cheerfulness and strong faith. Sweat was on the forehead, but a smile was on the lips. You were inspired and lifted up, and you walked away thinking that your own problems were not so bad after all.

James tells us what to do when affliction strikes: "Is any one among you suffering? Let him pray. Is any cheerful? Let him sing praise" (James 5: 13). He doesn't say we ought to tell the whole world how terrible we feel.

Then there is the instruction from Paul (who himself had more than his share of physical suffering) to the weakly young Timothy: "Share in suffering as a good soldier of Christ Jesus" (2 Timothy 2:3).

It's not easy to exhibit a beautiful tongue of peaceful trust when the body is being plagued with pain. It takes more than human power to grin and bear it. It takes the power of God's Holy Spirit. "I can do all things in him who strengthens me" (Philippians 4:13).

A Contented Tongue Disciplines Itself in the Face of Apparent Injustices

It's not easy to keep from complaining. Life just doesn't seem fair sometimes. You struggle along honestly, living moderately in order to stay within your income. Meanwhile, the fellow down the street operates a fraudulent air conditioner repair service and owns a swimming pool, three cars, a camper, a boat, and four color TV sets. Your teenage daughter, who is trying to lead a godly and chaste life, gets discouraged because her unprincipled classmates are getting the dates. Your son comes home with an honest C, and his classmates receive dishonest B's. No, it's not easy to keep from complaining.

When you're feeling low because of the apparent success of the dishonest and immoral people of the world, read Psalm 37. Often called "The Psalm for the Fretful," it reassures us that God is still a God of justice, and there is no wrong which will not eventually be made right: "Fret not yourself because of the wicked, be not envious of wrongdoers! For they will soon fade like the grass, and wither like the green herb (vv. 1, 2).

Are you tempted to complain to God? "Be still before the LORD, and wait patiently for him; fret not yourself over him who prospers in his way, over the man who carries out evil devices!" (vs. 7).

Are you tempted to lash out with your tongue in jealous anger? "Refrain from anger, and forsake wrath! Fret not yourself; it tends only to evil" (vs. 8).

A Contented Tongue Will Improve Your Church Life

In almost every church there are a number of members who are always, always, always complaining about something. On one particular Sunday morning after the service, two individuals in my church came up to one of the elders — one to tell him that I was preaching too long and the other to tell him that I wasn't preaching long enough!

Frankly, it gets very disheartening. It makes ministers less effective, and it has been known to send their wives away on vacations to mental institutions. It is discouraging to lay leaders of the church when the very people who always have an excuse for not helping are the same people who sit back and criticize those who finally volunteer to do the job. It is disillusioning to new Christians. They come vibrant and eager to work in the church organizations, expecting to be uplifted and inspired; but instead they find a thistle patch of griping and complaining.

The problem is that the very people who are the complainers, grumblers, and criticizers can't seem to recognize themselves. When they read an article like this, they are already pointing their finger at someone else. Perhaps at this point you should pause about five minutes to consider whether or not it is *you* I am talking about.

"Do all things without grumbling or questioning," says the scripture, "that you may be blameless and innocent, children of God without blemish in the midst of a crooked and perverse generation, among whom you shine as lights in the world" (Philippians 2:14, 15).

A Contented Tongue Will Improve Your Home Life

One who no doubt knew what he was talking about said: "It is better to live in a corner of a housetop than in a house shared with a contentious woman" (Proverbs 25:24).

"My husband doesn't hear a word I say," complains Constance Kelly. "He can read the evening paper, listen to a football game on radio, and watch a hockey game on television without missing a thing. But when I talk to him, it's like he's stone deaf."

There are many causes of this malady (which is almost as common as the common cold), and many husbands are simply too self-centered to talk with their wives as equals. But one of the causes of masculine silence in the home is the "nag virus." At first the hubby was willing and even eager to converse with his bride. Then it became apparent that her chief topic of conversation was an endless list of his inadequacies, his unfinished projects, the clothes she didn't have, and how the Van Snozzles had it better than they did. Soon he just turned her off and listened to more pleasant things.

Husbands aren't the only people who get nagged. Sons and daughter are next in line, chiefly over the way they dress, the manner in which they take care of their rooms, and their choice of friends. "I can do a hundred things right," one teenage girl complained bitterly, "but all I hear about is the few things I do wrong."

The way to cure the nag habit is to accentuate the positive. Complimenting a husband on how well he painted the kitchen will do more for a marriage than criticizing the way he didn't paint the bathroom (besides, the bathroom will probably get painted faster, too). Praising your children for their good habits will encourage them to overcome the bad ones.

Don't allow your family to get into the habit of complaining. Require your children to take a positive attitude toward their school work; don't allow them to become chronic complainers about their teachers and assignments. Require them to take a positive attitude toward the meals you serve; don't allow them to mumble under their breath about eating "this slop again" (yes, I have overheard this in a few homes). Require them to find an answer to each new problem as it emerges, rather than wringing their hands and complaining about how bad things are.

BEAUTY EXERCISES

1. Think of all the things you have criticized concerning your church, its leaders, and its pastor. Write them on a sheet of paper, being as specific as you can. Now, on the other side of the sheet, itemize all that you have done in a positive way to correct these faults. Which side of the sheet looks more impressive? After you have done this, vow not to do any more criticizing until you have done all within your power to remedy the situation. In other words, be a builder, not a wrecker.

2. Next time you are about to complain about something you don't have, stop and thank God for something you do have. Then ask a few questions about whatever it is you say is lacking. Is it a necessity or a luxury? How much would you actually use it if you had it? Do you want it because you really need it or because someone else has one like it? Could your money be spent more wisely on something else? What would it do to your stewardship toward the church and other Christian causes?

3. Be able to recite the "Breath Fresheners" which follow. If there are a few which are par-

ticularly appropriate for you, write them on cards and set them on the cupboard.

4. Read Psalm 37.

BREATH FRESHENERS
That Will Make You Nice to Be Near

First Week:

"There is great gain in godliness with contentment" (1 Timothy 6:6).

Second Week:

"I know how to be abased, and I know how to abound; in any and all circumstances I have learned the secret of facing plenty and hunger, abundance and want. I can do all things in him who strengthens me" (Philippians 4:12, 13).

Third Week:

"Fret not yourself because of the wicked, be not envious of wrongdoers!" (Psalm 37:1).

Fourth Week:

"It is better to live in a corner of the housetop than in a house shared with a contentious woman" (Proverbs 25:24).

BEAUTY HINT #10
A Beautiful Tongue
Is a Simple Tongue

"Simple" is defined in the dictionary as "without ostentation," "unpretending," "natural," "not ornate," "unembellished." A beautifully simple tongue is one which makes no effort to impress, to flatter, to embellish, to exaggerate. It does not try to give the impression that the speaker is richer, wiser, holier, or greater then she really is.

Jesus was a simple man. He made no effort to "make an impression." He wore no clothes that drew special attention to Himself. He made no effort to be seen socializing with the "right" people.

Jesus spoke in simple words. He drew parables and analogies from the common things of life, like mustard seeds and sheepfolds. He didn't try to "tone down" His more pointed remarks. He didn't use obscure words or intellectual-sounding phrases. As a result, the common people heard Him gladly.

The Apostle Paul believed he should follow the example of his Master in this respect. He came preaching, he says, "not with eloquent wisdom, lest the cross of Christ be emptied of its power" (1 Corinthians 1:17). Then he goes on to say that the simple, unembellished truth of God is far more effective in saving the world than all the fancy wisdom of the world:

> But God chose what is foolish in the world to shame the wise, God chose what is weak in

the world to shame the strong, God chose what is low and despised in the world, even things that are not, to bring to nothing things that are, so that no human being might boast in the presence of God (1 Corinthians 1: 27-29).

A Simple Tongue Uses a Simple Yes or No

Jesus said, "Do not swear at all, either by heaven . . . or by the earth . . . or by Jerusalem. . . . (or) by your head. . . . Let what you say be simply 'Yes' or 'No'; anything more than this comes from evil" (Matthew 5:34-37).

This "swearing" does not necessarily refer to profanity. It refers to the making of oaths in order to convince somebody you are telling the truth. The point is that others should be able to assume your truthfulness on the basis of your character. There should be no need to substantiate your words with all sorts of fancy expressions like "by God," "I'll swear on a stack of Bibles," or the childish, "cross my heart and hope to die, stick a needle in my eye." Establish such a reputation for having a truthful tongue (remember chapter 8?) that you can boldly use a simple tongue.

A Simple Tongue Avoids Flattery

Gushers are welcome only on oil fields. And even there they are quickly capped.

Remember the old peacock with the huge hat who went around crooning "Isn't it absolutely divine," "How mar-velous," and "Oh, Martha, this is the most heavenly party!" It was well-intentioned, perhaps, and meant to show appreciation, but it was overdone. And when compliments become overdone, they lose both their sincerity and credibility.

One of the many wise sayings in the Book of Proverbs is this one: "It is not good to eat much honey, so be sparing of complimentary words" (Proverbs 25:27). Most people like to eat honey — but only a little at a time. Too often and too much gets sickening. Most people also like to hear compliments — but only a few at a time. Too often and too much gets sickening.

Let's be honest. Many of our compliments are meant more to impress other people than they are to express how we are impressed by them. Then it becomes flattery, and flattery is a form of a lie.

When you appreciate something, say it (see Chapter 3); but say it simply, briefly, and sincerely.

A Simple Tongue Avoids Exaggeration

Titus 2:7 says that in our teaching we are to display "integrity, gravity, and sound speech."

If the incident you are telling your friends about was funny, there is no need to try to make it funnier. If the fish you caught was twelve inches long, tell them it was twelve inches long. If you had an operation last year, there is no need to make it sound worse than it was (if, indeed, you must describe it at all). If your children are intelligent, that fact will be obvious to all and you won't have to conjure up a story about how their teachers praise them. If you find yourself in a certain economic bracket, what good will it do to try to give the impression that you are in a higher one?

A Simple Tongue Uses
Simple Language With God

"Holy and infinite Jehovah, we beseech thee," drones the minister, "look down upon us, Thy humble servants, in Thine infinite mercy and with Thy ineffable love. . . ."

That's the kind of pastoral prayer that many of us are used to. There is a certain dignity and beauty about such language in prayer, but we pose some questions. Are dignity and beauty the objectives of prayer? Does the use of high-sounding words increase the effectiveness of the prayer? Do they encourage others to lead in public prayer? Who are we trying to impress — people or God? Or, perhaps, isn't prayer meant to impress anyone?

Jesus advocated simplicity in prayer. He said, "And in praying do not heap up empty phrases as the Gentiles do; for they think that they will be heard for their many words" (Matthew 6:7). Then He proceeded to teach His followers a model prayer which is the epitome of directness and simplicity. There is no fluff, no fancy language in the Lord's Prayer — just simple praise and direct petition.

The effective prayer for forgiveness uttered by the publican was only seven words long. Paul prayed for the removal of the thorn in his flesh, not ten times or a hundred times, but only three times.

The best way to pray is in a way which for you is natural, normal, and sincere.

BEAUTY EXERCISES
To Eliminate Unnecessary Flab

1. One day during your private prayers, do this. First, pray in your customary way. Then try to write down exactly what you said. Pick out the words you have repeated so often they have become trite and meaningless. Substitute fresher and plainer words. For instance, if you use "be-

seech," try using "ask" or "request" instead. If you use "trespasses," say "wrongs" or "sins."

2. Lead a prayer in Bible Study, in Sunday school, or in some other organization without using flowery language or impressive phrases.

3. Relate a humorous incident that happened to you last week without exaggerating even one small detail.

4. If you like her new dress, tell her so. If not, don't say anything.

5. Suppress the temptation to use a newly learned big word to impress your Friday night guests.

6. Give a compliment to someone from whom you have nothing to gain.

BREATH FRESHENERS

First Week:
"Let what you say be simply 'Yes' or 'No'; anything more than this comes from evil" (Matthew 5:37).

Second Week:
"It is not good to eat much honey, so be sparing of complimentary words" (Proverbs 25:27).

Third Week:
"And in praying do not heap up empty phrases as the Gentiles do; for they think that they will be heard for their many words" (Matthew 6:7).

Fourth Week:
"(Love) is not possessive: it is neither anxious to impress nor does it cherish inflated ideas of its own importance" (1 Corinthians 13:4, Phillips).

Leader's Guide

for a study of
Beauty Care for the Tongue

NOTES TO THE GROUP LEADER

General Preparation

In this brief space we cannot begin to tell you how to become a good group leader for your Bible study. Many volumes have been written on how to become a better teacher, how to lead a discussion, how to be a leader of small groups, and how to develop other leadership skills. Let us simply say that you should make use of all the opportunities you have in order to prepare yourself in a general way for the task of Bible study leadership. Attend seminars, participate in Sunday school conventions, read books, and — most important of all — learn from experience.

Not One Method

Nor are we going to tell you how you should present this material. Some will want to teach it by the lecture method. Some will do it almost entirely by discussion. Some will want to use role-play situations or small groups. May we suggest that the best method is a variety of methods. No matter what you may be doing, it will get tiresome if you do it the same way all the time.

What This Guide Contains

This guide is not meant to be comprehensive. We hope you will go to other sources for additional material. However, we have included here a number of items which we hope will be helpful in leading a group study of the "Beauty Care" material. You will find such things as:

1. *Suggestions* on how to introduce or present the topic. Lesson 1, for instance, contains a "Quickie Poll" which can be used to excite interest in the topic and give the leader helpful information.

2. *What others have said* — quotable quotes on the subject, which you may use with your other material as you see fit.

3. *Discussion questions.* You will think of others, no doubt, but these will give you a start.

4. *Illustrations* so that you can have some "original" items to add to your presentation.

5. *Additional material,* to supplement the main text.

6. *Additional scripture references* to supplement those used in the lesson and the "Breath Fresheners."

Additional Resource Materials

Please do not be content with what we have given you. Consult resource books for additional material. Browse in your city and church libraries. Talk it over with your husband or a friend. Don't be afraid to ask for help from your pastor. He probably has much helpful material in his files as well as useful books in his library. Some sources:

Commentaries on the Bible verses mentioned
Bible dictionaries
Books of illustrations
Practical and inspirational books for women, such as those by Eugenia Price
Books of quotations

Also, keep your eyes and ears open for current materials which illustrate the subject. This means you must preview the lessons some time beforehand so you know what to look for. Check with:

Newspaper stories
Magazine articles and fiction
Novels
Comments made by friends and neighbors
Personal incidents in your own life

Using the Beauty Exercises

Each month's lesson includes a number of "Beauty Exercises," practical suggestions on how the participants can put into practice the principles suggested in the study. These can provide a wealth of material for discussion. For instance, ask Mary L. if she has tried Beauty Exercise No. 3 and how well she did with it.

Using the Breath Fresheners

Each month's lesson also includes four "Breath Fresheners" — four Bible verses which can be most valuable if they are committed to memory. Memorization is valuable, because in the process of learning and repeating, the meaning can become deeply immersed in the soul. You can encourage the memorization of these verses by: (1) suggesting that they memorize a new verse each week and at the same time review all previous verses; (2) Demonstrating to them how you have written verses on 3x5 cards and carry them with you for frequent reference; and (3) Having the group repeat the verses in unison at the monthly meeting. Perhaps this can be done as a concluding act of worship at the meeting, with everyone standing.

The Importance of a Beautiful Tongue

Quickie Poll

Stir interest in the subject and gain pertinent information by taking a quickie poll of the group. Mimeograph the questionnaire below, have the participants fill them out early in the meeting (unsigned, of course), and have a helper compile the results for you while the meeting is in progress. Report the results to the group as a part of your lesson presentation (a chalkboard may help). You may also wish to use the compiled statistics as a springboard for discussion.

1. I have trouble controlling my tongue (a) never, (b) seldom, (c) sometimes, (d) frequently.

2. After an argument, I usually feel that I was most hurt by (a) the issues that were involved, or (b) the words that were said.

3. As to gossip, I feel that I am (a) never, (b) seldom, (c) sometimes, (d) frequently guilty.

4. During this past week I was able to use my tongue constructively by

_____ comforting a child.　　_____ witnessing for Christ.
_____ expressing love to　　_____ defending a good
my husband.　　　　　　　cause.
_____ advising a friend.　　_____ expressing sympathy
and concern.

5. Generally, I believe I talk (a) too much, (b) too little, or (c) about the right amount.

71

6. Check the faulty uses of the tongue that bother you most in other people (mark three). *

_____ Too talkative	_____ Unkind
_____ Unappreciative	_____ Gossipy
_____ Never witnessing	_____ Lying
_____ Filthy	_____ Exaggerating
_____ Complaining	

The Human Tongue Is Distinctive

Some animals have fancier tongues than humans do. Snakes and lizards have forked tongues which also serve as organs of smell. Teeth grow on the tongues of some fish, such as the salmon and trout. Frogs, toads, and chameleons have very long tongues which can dart out with blinding speed to capture insects.

Although our human tongues cannot harpoon a dinner, bite, or smell, they can do something even more fantastic — they can form words. This is one of the abilities which makes us distinctive from the animal world, and this is one of the abilities which gives us such a tremendous potential for both good and evil.

What Others Have Said

"The tongue is, at the same time, the best part of man and his worst; with good government, none is more useful, and without it, none is more mischievous" (Anarcharsis).

"It is observed in the course of worldly things, that man's fortunes are oftener made by their tongues than by their virtues; and more men's fortunes overthrown thereby than by vices" (Sir Walter Raleigh).

---

* Note: These nine choices are the nine topics covered in the book.

"How often you are irresistibly drawn to a plain, unassuming woman, whose soft silvery tones render her positively attractive! In the social circle, how pleasant it is to hear a woman talk in that low key which always characterizes the true lady. In the sanctuary of home, how such a voice soothes the fretful child and cheers the weary husband!" (Charles Lamb).

Isaiah's Tongue

Isaiah 6:1-8 relates the story of how God called Isaiah to become a prophet. He did so by first giving Isaiah a vision of His awesome holiness and then by sanctifying the prophet's tongue. Isaiah realized, after catching a glimpse of the purity of God, that his tongue needed to be purified: "Woe is me! For I am lost; for I am a man of unclean lips, and I dwell in the midst of a people of unclean lips" (vs. 5). Then the angel touched the prophet's lips with a burning coal taken from the fire, a token of forgiveness and restoration (and perhaps a hint about how painful it is to cleanse the tongue): "Behold, this has touched your lips; your guilt is taken away, and your sin is forgiven" (vs. 7). Then, and only then, was Isaiah ready for service: "And I heard the voice of the Lord saying, 'Whom shall I send, and who will go for us?' Then I said, 'Here am I! Send me'" (vs. 8).

Truth: When we become aware of the holiness of God, we become aware of how much our tongues need to be cleansed.

Truth: In order to be ready to serve, we must let God cleanse our tongues.

Judgment and the Tongue

At the end of the age, we will be judged by how we have used our tongues. Said Jesus, "I tell you, on the day of judgment men will render account of every careless word they utter; for by your words you will be justified, and by your words you will be condemned" (Matthew 12:36, 37). The tongue reveals more about a person than almost anything else does. Although for a time the tongue may "cover up," it eventually reveals the truth about character. Like the mouth of a babbling spring, it reveals the nature of the water's source. "The good man out of his good treasure brings forth good, and the evil man out of his evil treasure brings forth evil" (Matthew 12:35).

A Beautiful Tongue
Is a Silent Tongue

Three Discussion Ideas

1. List the four benefits of constructive silence on a chalkboard as you introduce them. Ask the group members to suggest additional benefits and add them to the list. Have some of your own and be ready to contribute them.

2. Discuss how practical this rule might be for your homes: "If you can't find anything nice to say about a person, don't say it." (Some families have established this as a rule for mealtimes.) What are its advantages? Disadvantages? How important is the parents' example?

3. We have spoken in this lesson about "constructive silence," implying that there may be other kinds. Can silence be used destructively as well as constructively? Which is worse, the noisy argument or the "silent treatment"?

An Additional Reason for Keeping Silent

There is an additional reason for keeping silent: by saying nothing, you hide your ignorance! There is an old saying, "By saying nothing, you may pass as wise." This was probably inspired by Proverbs 17:28: "Even a fool who keeps silent is considered wise; when he closes his lips, he is deemed intelligent." When you don't know what you are talking about, it's far better to hide your ignorance than to prove it beyond reasonable doubt!

Illustrations

You can, we are sure, make the topic more interesting and amusing by telling an anecdote or two from your own experience — perhaps how you "stuck your foot in your mouth" or embarrassed yourself in some other way by talking too much.

What Others Have Said

"Woman's tongue is her sword, which she never lets rust" (Madame Necker).

"The tongue should not be allowed to outrun the mind" (Chilo).

"Speech is silver; silence is golden" (German Proverb).

"Speech is the art of stifling and suspending thought" (Carlyle).

"We rarely repent of speaking little, but often of speaking too much" (Bruyere).

"Half of the sorrows of women would be averted if they could repress the speech they know to be useless — nay, the speech they have resolved not to utter" (George Eliot).

How to Be a Good Listener

Here are some suggestions on how to become a more effective "sounding board" for others:

1. Be able to keep a confidence. Never, never spread to someone else something which has been told you in confidence, even though you introduce it with, "Don't pass this on to anyone else. . . ."

2. Don't feel compelled to express agreement or disagreement with every statement made.

3. Refrain from belittling her problems by telling about yours.

4. Be slow to give advice. Your friend, by "talking it through" with you, will probably be able to come to her own decision.

5. Ask questions which will help her understand herself, such as "Why do you feel that way?" and "You've changed your opinion about that, haven't you?"

6. Be able to keep a confidence. (Yes, I know I said it once before.)

Additional Verses for Study and Comment

"When words are many, transgression is not lacking, but he who restrains his lips is prudent" (Proverbs 10:19).

"He (Pilate) entered the praetorium again and said to Jesus, 'Where are you from?' But Jesus gave no answer" (John 19:9).

Attention!

Prepare for your next topic, "A Beautiful Tongue Is an Appreciative Tongue," by asking the ladies to be especially appreciative to others throughout the month. See No. 1 under next month's "Beauty Exercises."

Long-Winded Speakers

According to the *Guinness Book of World Records*, 1974 edition, the longest sermon on record is 48 hours, 18 minutes, delivered by Clinton Locy of West Richland, Washington, in February, 1955. (And you think your minister gets long-winded sometimes!)

A Beautiful Tongue
Is an Appreciative Tongue

Reports From the Floor

At the previous meeting, ask the ladies to take special note of "Beauty Exercise" No. 1. Ask them to make a special effort throughout the month to express appreciation to the people who serve them in various ways. Have them report at this meeting how they did — who they spoke to, how they said it, and what the response was (shock, disbelief, rejection, smile, etc.). This may prove to be the most valuable part of your study hour.

What Others Have Said

"To appreciate the noble is a gain which can never be torn from us" (Goethe).

"By appreciation we make excellence in others our own property" (Voltaire).

"To praise great actions with sincerity may be said to be taking part in them" (Rochefoucauld).

"We are very much what others think of us. The reception our observations meet with gives us courage to proceed or dampens our efforts" (Hazlitt).

Additional Point

In addition to the four things an appreciative tongue will do, as covered in the main text, you may add a fifth: *An appreciative tongue can strengthen your character*.

Appreciation leads to imitation. We tend to become like that which we admire. A now-obscure fellow named Lavater once said, "He is incapable of a truly good action who knows not the pleasure in contemplating the good actions of others."

He who truly appreciates generosity is more likely to become a generous person. He who truly appreciates beauty in art will be motivated to create his own beauty. To truly appreciate Jesus Christ for His self-giving love is at the same time to seek to adopt His character as your own lifestyle.

Discussion Ideas

1. When commenting on "An Appreciative Tongue Will Put Your Requests into Perspective," you may wish to discuss whether this same principle carries over into person-to-person relationships. There is, for instance, a thankful way and a thankless way of asking for things: "John, we need a new davenport and chair. I'm so embarrassed when we have people over to have them see this old piece of junk." Or, "John, we need a new davenport and chair set. We've had good use from our old one because you bought a good set, but I'm afraid that time has caught up with it." It's more than a matter of tact. It's a matter of appreciation. Remember, an appreciative tongue is a beautful tongue.

2. When commenting on "An Appreciative Tongue Will Give You a Better Home Life," you might ask for discussion on whether parents also should make a special point of appreciating their children. Is it possible that thanklessness on the part of children may be partially caused by parents who have failed to appreciate them? Is it true

that children become what you say they are? Try to get specific examples and experiences.

Additional Verses for Study and Comment

"Let there be no filthiness, nor silly talk, nor levity, which are not fitting; but instead let there be thanksgiving" (Ephesians 5:4).

"And whatever you do, in word or deed, do everything in the name of the Lord Jesus, giving thanks to God the Father through him" (Colossians 3:17).

"Then I will thank thee in the great congregation; in the mighty throng I will praise thee" (Psalm 35:18).

"And he took the cup, and when he had given thanks he gave it to them, and they all drank of it" (Mark 14:23).

"And when he had said this, he took bread, and giving thanks to God in the presence of all he broke it and began to eat" (Acts 27:35).

A Beautiful Tongue
Is a Witnessing Tongue

Christmas Tie-in

In Luke 2:20 we read, "And the shepherds returned, glorifying and praising God for all they had heard and seen, as it had been told them." The shepherds immediately became witnesses to others. They were so overwhelmed by the Good News they had received and experienced that they couldn't possibly refrain from telling everybody about it. They didn't wait until they knew all the facts and theological implications; they didn't wait until they had been trained by the experts; they didn't care whether or not people would call them "fanatics." They just told it as they had seen it, forcefully, thankfully, and immediately.

Discussion Ideas

Evangelism has been defined as "one beggar telling another beggar where to find bread." Discuss the implications of this statement, especially as it relates to:

(a) The urgency of the message
(b) The humility of the messenger
(c) The naturalness of the situation

Additional Verses for Study and Comment

"But Peter and John answered them, 'Whether it is right in the sight of God to listen to you rather than to God, you must judge; for we cannot but speak of what we have seen and heard'" (Acts 4:19, 20).

"That which we have seen and heard we proclaim to you, so that you may have fellowship with us; and our fellowship is with the Father and with his Son Jesus Christ" (1 John 1:3).

"For I am not ashamed of the gospel" (Romans 1:16).

Evangelism Training Programs

You may wish to introduce one or more of the major programs for training lay people how to be effective witnesses for Christ. Many groups have developed fine techniques and materials during the past years. It is possible that people who have been trained in these evangelism programs are living in your area and are available to speak. You can contact the headquarters of these groups and ask for information. Here are a few you may wish to contact; perhaps your pastor will recommend others.

> Lay Witness Mission
> The Institute of Church Renewal, Inc.
> 1610 LaVista Road, Northeast
> Atlanta, Georgia 30329

> "Evangelism Explosion"
> Coral Ridge Presbyterian Church
> 5550 N. Federal Highway
> Ft. Lauderdale, Fla. 33308

> The Navigators
> Colorado Springs, Colorado 80900

> Lay Institute for Evangelism
> Campus Crusade for Christ International
> Arrowhead Springs
> San Bernadino, California 92400

A Beautiful Tongue
Is a Clean Tongue

Illustration

You may wish to use this illustration to emphasize the holiness of the name of God.

Sometimes when an outstanding athlete graduates from a college or retires from a career in his sport, his number is "retired." For instance, if his suit number was 12, no one in the future will wear number 12. It is set apart for him alone as a token of high esteem and honor. No other athlete will share the glory of that number.

Similarly, the name of God has been "retired," as well as the names for Jesus Christ and the Holy Spirit. No one else can use it. His name is for His exclusive use. It is a "holy" (literally, "set apart") name, to be treated with reverence and honor. "I am the LORD, that is my name," says God. "My glory I give to no other" (Isaiah 42:8).

Additional Point

You may wish to add an additional point to the ones developed in the main text: *A clean tongue refuses to use filthy talk.*

"Let there be no filthiness, nor silly talk, nor levity, which are not fitting," says Ephesians 5:4.

X-rated movies have been around for a few years, but X-rated tongues have wagged since earliest history.

Children readily pass on "dirty stories" to their friends and classmates with great gusto, proving how daring they are.

Many adults never grow out of that stage. To the end of their lives they are "proving" their sophistication or cleverness or sensuousness by repeating the same old dog-eared tales. There are some new ones, of course, supplied by many of the "men's" magazines on the market, but they are really retreads of the old ones.

What should you do about the dirty stories and off-color jokes you hear? Sometimes you can't help but hear them, you know. The words of Jesus are appropriate: "Not what goes into the mouth defiles a man, but what comes out of the mouth, this defiles a man" (Matthew 15:11). You become defiled when you try to remember the story and pass it on. You don't have to act shocked or laugh nervously; simply throw in a disgusted or pitying glance and forget it.

Discussion Ideas

1. Does your group agree or disagree with the following statements? Why?

"The use of profanity reflects a poverty of vocabulary rather than a richness of intelligence."

"Profanity is man's lowest substitute for wit."

"You can tell the size of a man by the size of the thing that makes him swear."

2. Does the stipulation of the third commandment include the various names for Jesus and the Holy Spirit, as well as the names of God the Father? Why?

3. What about the slang words that are a little different from the holy names but sound very much

like them? For instance, should the Christian use "gosh," "jeez," "gee," etc.?

4. What about the excuse commonly given for swearing: "It's only a habit"? Are we responsible for habits? How do habits originate? Are there good habits and bad habits? Are good deeds less praiseworthy because they are repeated often and have become habitual? Are bad deeds less blameworthy because they are repeated often and have become habitual?

5. The Lord's Prayer is compact, crowding into a few words the basic essentials of good prayer. It includes the phrase, "hallowed be thy name." Is this an indication of how important the third commandment is?

Looking Ahead to Hint #6

See item No. 6 of the "Beauty Exercises" in the next lesson. You may wish to make the assignment at the close of this meeting. Refer also to the paraphrase of 1 Corinthians 13:3 which appears in the next chapter of this leader's guide.

BEAUTY HINT #6

A Beautiful Tongue
Is a Kind Tongue

The Devastating Power of an Unkind Tongue

According to *World Book Encyclopedia* about
3,000,000 acres of trees are destroyed by fire in the
United States every year. About half of these are
caused by nature (lightning); the rest are caused
by man. The chief causes of forest fires (in order
of frequency) are brush or trash fires which get
out of hand, arson, and negligent smokers.

The point is that almost all of these devastating
fires are caused by a very small fire or even by a
single spark. The fire on one leaf quickly spreads
to the branch and thence to the tree and surround-
ing trees. Thus it is with the fires set by the
tongue. Recrimination follows recrimination, and
insult follows insult. What begins as a small criticism of one aspect of the person ("Your hair looks
lousy.") soon envelopes the entire personality ("I
should have listened to my mother and never married you.").

Who knows how many of our blazing racial
troubles were ignited years ago when the undisciplined and hate-filled words of a white person
lodged in the mind of a young black, smoldering
there for years until it erupted in a fire of violence?

Who knows how many divorces have been
caused because one spark of uncontrolled tongue-

fire was allowed to rampage unchecked through the lives of a husband, wife, and even children, devouring all that was happy and holy?

For "A Kind Tongue Helps to Make a House a Home" (Supplementary)

In Bunyan's *Pilgrim's Progress* one of the feminine characters, Talkative, is described as "a saint abroad and a devil at home."

Do you want to make your teenagers bitter against Christianity? One sure way is to talk like a saint at church and lash out like a devil at home. Teenagers see something terribly inconsistent in the mother who speaks with impressive sweetness when she leads the guild devotions and then at home calls her children a "bunch of brats" before she runs to the phone to tell the world what an awful dress Julia Sparrow was wearing.

Supplementary Material for "A Kind Tongue Promotes Peace"

"A soft answer," says one of the Proverbs, "turns away wrath" (15:1).

A soft answer is a quiet answer. As the old Indian is reported to have advised the young brave and his new squaw, "Never raise voice unless wigwam is on fire."

A soft answer is also a non-argumentative answer. It may defend, but it does not lash back. It may stand stoutly for the truth, but it does not criticize.

A soft answer is not a weak answer or a powerless answer. It is, in fact, the *strongest* kind of answer because it has the capability of subduing one of mankind's most vicious weapons — an angry tongue.

Supplementary Material for
"A Kind Tongue Is a Positive Witness"

Colossians 4:5, 6 says that our speech is to be "seasoned with salt." Salt does two things: it preserves and it makes things more palatable. It doesn't really change the food, but it makes it more pleasant to the taste. It makes the difference between eating food and enjoying food. Likewise, graciousness does not necessarily change the contents of the message we bring, but it does make it more acceptable, pleasant, and believable.

Discussion Ideas

1. Discuss how a loving tongue is involved in keeping each of the Ten Commandments. Love, after all, is a summary of the entire Law. For instance, honoring your father and your mother involves speaking to them in a particular way.

2. Where is it most difficult to be kind? At home? At church? At work? Why? Under what circumstances are you most likely to be unkind?

Paraphrase of 1 Corinthians 13

See suggestion No. 6 of the "Beauty Exercises" in the main text, which suggests that the members of the group try to write their own versions of 1 Corinthians 13. They can try the first three verses or, if they wish, do the entire chapter. Some suggestions: "A housewife's version," "A Sunday school teacher's version," "A church member's version," etc.

Eternity magazine published such a paraphrase by this author, * and we quote part of that article to give you an idea of the possibilities.

---

* "The Indispensable Ingredient," *Eternity*, April, 1970, pp. 15-17.

"If I give away all I have, and if I deliver my body to be burned, but have not love, I gain nothing" (1 Corinthians 13:3).

"If I give my children all the toys they could ask for, and if I deliver my automobile for my teenager to use every night, but have not love, I gain nothing."

"If I give my husband a clean home and good meals, but have not love, I gain nothing."

"If I give away all I have to the poverty program, and if I deliver my body to be sacrificed on a civil rights march, but have not love, I gain nothing."

"If I make a generous pledge to the church, and if I deliver up my old clothing to the rescue mission, but lovelessly grumble about it, I am nothing."

"If I give generous presents at Christmas in an effort to keep up with what others will give me, but have not love, I gain nothing."

Ask some of the ladies to read their versions before the group. You may even want to publish some of the better ones in your church newsletter.

A Beautiful Tongue Is a Tongue That Does Not Gossip

A Gossip Book

Suggest that your study group begin a gossip-book project. (Present this very seriously, tongue in cheek of course, and see what kind of comments you get.) Tell them you will provide a notebook with blank pages. If they have a criticism or complaint against someone or have heard a story about someone, write it in this book and sign it. You will then bring the book to that person, have her read it, and bring back a written reply on the same page.

Small Group Discussion

Divide into small groups and have each group think of as many harmful effects of gossip as they can. Set a time limit of about 10 minutes. After the entire group is together again, have one person report for each group and record the ideas on a chalkboard. A few ideas:

A negative witness for Christ
Harmful to the reputation of others
Conveys a bad example to children
Is an offense against love
Cannot be retrieved
Violates the commandment about false witness
Is hypocrisy; nice to the face, nasty to the back.

"Gossip is like mud thrown against a clean wall; it may not stick, but it leaves a mark."

"The difference between gossip and news is whether you hear it or tell it."

"There are male as well as female gossips" (Colton).

"Everyone says it, and what everybody says must be true" (James Fenimore Cooper).

"Old gossips are usually young flirts gone to seed" (J. L. Basford).

"Female gossips are generally actuated by active ignorance" (Rochefaucauld).

"Guess What They'll Say Next"

Announce that you are going to conduct a quiz. You will give some commonly heard statements ending with the word "but," and the participants must supply the last part of the sentence.

1. "I'm not one to gossip, but ⸻ "
2. "Don't get me wrong; I'm not a bigot, and some of them are my best friends, but ⸻ "
3. "I don't mean to imply that Jean isn't doing a good job as committee chairman, but ⸻ "
4. "I don't mean to be critical of the way you handled the situation, but ⸻ "
5. "Jim is a fine husband in many ways, but ⸻ "

The point is that the very statements we use to excuse our gossiping are the statements that give us away. Whenever you hear someone say, "I'm not . . . but . . . ," you can be sure that no good will come from it.

Discussion Idea

Discuss some possible cures for gossiping. A few

have been suggested by the "Five Reasons for Gossiping": gain self-confidence in a more wholesome way; find more important things to do, etc. You might try small group discussions with this one.

BEAUTY HINT #8
A Beautiful Tongue
Is a Truthful Tongue

Half-truths

When discussing "A Truthful Tongue Avoids Half-Truths," point out that Satan used the half-truth ruse when he tempted Adam and Eve. "For God knows that when you eat of it your eyes will be opened, and you will be like God, knowing good and evil" (Genesis 3:5), he said. This was partially correct, of course, because they would come to know evil as well as good. But the other part of the statement, that they would be like God, was a lie.

Discussion Ideas

1. To what extent do you think we lie when we sing some of our church hymns? For instance, "I'll Go Where You Want Me to Go," "All for Jesus," and "Take My Life and Let It Be." If we don't mean it, should we keep on singing anyway?

2. Discuss the possible results of telling small untruths to our children. Perhaps you or others can relate some personal experiences which are relevant. What effects will it have on our children? On us?

3. Do you believe that lie-telling can become habitual? Perhaps you are acquainted with people who lie even when they don't have to.

Role-play

The situation: Mary has just had an operation

for the removal of a tumor. Her sister, Jane, tells her the truth — that the tumor was not malignant. Mary's husband, however, died of cancer a few years ago, and until the end Mary told him that he didn't have cancer. Therefore she will not believe Jane.

Appoint a Mary and a Jane to role-play the situation, then discuss what can be done to solve the problem and to avoid such situations in the future.

You may be able to think of other "plots" to act out and discuss in a similar manner. A few are suggested in the paragraph in the main text on "White Lies."

What Others Have Said About Truth

"Truth needs no flowers of speech" (Pope).

"How sweet the words of truth breathed from the lips of love" (James Beattie).

"Don't be 'consistent,' but be simply true"
(Holmes).

"Peace, if possible, but the truth at any rate" (Martin Luther).

"Beware of a half-truth; you may get hold of the wrong half."

"The sting of reproach is the truth of it" (Benjamin Franklin).

"Any time you find that truth stands in your way, you may be sure that you are headed in the wrong direction."

"Nothing ruins the truth like stretching it."

"There are three sides to every story: your side, my side, and the truth."

Small-Group Discussions

In this day of many "liberation" movements, it might be instructive to divide into small groups and discuss the implications of John 8:32: "You will know the truth, and the truth will make you free." What does this teach about true freedom? What, if anything, does this teaching of Jesus have to do with racial liberation? Women's liberation? Political liberation?

A Beautiful Tongue Is a Contented Tongue

What Others Have Said

"A contented person is one who enjoys the scenery along the detour."

"Content makes poor men rich; discontent makes rich men poor" (Benjamin Franklin). (Change the gender as you read it; it will make it much more personal for the ladies.)

"When you feel dog-tired at night, it may be because you growled all day."

"Enjoy your own life without comparing it with that of another" (Condorcet).

"The usual fortune of complaint is to excite contempt more than pity" (Samuel Johnson).

"Those who complain most are most to be complained of" (Matthew Henry).

"Constant complaint is the poorest sort of pay for all the comforts we enjoy" (Benjamin Franklin).

"If Only. . . ."

A certain two-word prefix is among the most futile and senseless phrases in the English language. That phrase is "if only."

"If only I were beautiful. . . ."

"If only you had a better job. . . ."

"If only we had a boat/dishwasher/pool/larger home/etc. . . ."

"If only we didn't have so many children. . . ."

"If only we had more children. . . ."

"If only I had married someone else. . . ."

To go through life with an "if only" attitude is like driving a car with your eye constantly on the rear view mirror. You see where you *could have* turned off on a beautiful nature trail; you see where you *could have* stopped at a gas station; you see where you *missed* a beautiful rock formation, but you fail to see the opportunities ahead of you. Instead of complaining about the past, let us press on to the future. "Forgetting what lies behind and straining forward to what lies ahead, I press on toward the goal for the prize of the upward call of God in Christ Jesus" (Philippians 3:13, 14).

Illustration (Nagging)

Perhaps you have heard of the fellow who went into the restaurant one morning and ordered cold coffee, burnt toast, and an egg hard-boiled until it turned green. "Anything else?" asked the waitress, a bit confused. "Yes," said the man. "Please sit down here and nag me. I'm homesick."

Frankly, men don't get homesick for nagging wives any more than they get homesick for burnt toast and green eggs. The nagged husband is far more likely to make a different request of the waitress!

Sick Joke

"Why are women like angels?"

"Because they are always harping on something."

Small Group Discussion

Have your small groups discuss this one: "What are the secrets of a contented tongue?"

BEAUTY HINT #10

A Beautiful Tongue
Is a Simple Tongue

Discussion for "Simple Yes or No"

Ask the group to suggest other semi-profane expressions which are commonly used to bolster statements and to make them more impressive, such as "hell, no," and "for heaven's sake."

Additional Point: A Simple Tongue Doesn't Try to Impress Others by Its Speech.

There are many ways of trying to impress others by your use of the tongue:

— Talk with authority about books you haven't read (you read the reviews).

— Speak nonchalantly about how much your husband loses when the stock market goes down two cents a share.

— Use long, obscure, important-sounding words.

— Slip in a few slang expressions common among teenagers.

— Quote at length what some important person told you (actually, you were in the audience).

— Repeat as your own some judgment made by an authority in the field.

— Mention on frequent occasion that you are a tither and that you spend hours a day in prayer.

Love, says the Bible, "is neither anxious to impress nor does it cherish inflated ideas of its own importance" (1 Corinthians 13:4, Phillips). Truly loving speech is simple speech.

Discussion Idea

Name additional ways in which people try to impress others by the way they talk. Is this also done in the area of religion? Remember the scribes and the Pharisees praying on the street corners.

Simple Language in Prayer

Discuss with your group how they feel about the use of theological language in prayers. Ask some of the questions raised in the main text. Is there a difference between "beautiful" language and "flowery" language? Should the style of praying be different in private prayers than in public prayers? Should women who pray audibly at Bible study meetings feel they should follow a certain established pattern? Which should we use when addressing God — "Thee" and "Thou" or "You"?

Exaggeration Illustration

At a rally in Washington a few years ago, the clergyman-leader of the rally estimated that the crowd was 75,000. The police estimated it at 15,000. That's a 500 percent difference in opinion. Some Christian leaders have so consistently practiced the art of exaggeration that the term "evangelist's estimate" has been coined to describe any wildly overblown guess.

Prayer Books

Purchase or borrow any of the many books of private prayers which have been published in recent years. Many of these are very "chummy" in their approach to God. Read a few of the prayers to the group and ask for their comments.

Scripture Index

NOTES

NOTES